Wild Horses: A Denver Broncos Story

The Elway Era Through Today

RD Braaten

Table of Contents

Wild Horses - A Denver Broncos Story - Elway Through Today	1
New Franchise and a Jump to the 1980s	5
The Establishment of the Denver Broncos	5
The 1980's	6
Dan Reeves	6
Concluding the 80's and Summarizing the Reeves Era	9
ELWAY	11
1983 - Big Year for Many Reasons	12
Early Years and Early Success	13
The 90's	16
Mike Shanahan and Terrell Davis	19
Terrell Davis	22
1996	23
Late 20th Century Broncos Football	27
1997 Playoffs	29
Super Bowl : Green Bay Packers vs. Denver Broncos 1997 Season, Date: January 25th, 1998	31
CHAMPS - The Top of the Mountain!	34
1998 and Saying Goodbye	37
Playoffs - 1998	40
Super Bowl XXXIII January 31st, 1999	43
Retirement / Last Ride	44
Moving into the New Millennium	46

Terrell Davis Legacy	48
That Didn't Last Long	49
New Hope with the Snake	51
Jay Cutler	54
New Direction / The Break-Up	55
2010's and beyond	59
Peyton Manning Years	60
Playoffs 2013	66
AFC Title Game vs. the Patriots	67
Super Bowl XLVIII	67
2015	69
Playoffs 2015	71
Super Bowl 50! Date: February 7th, 2016 Santa Clara, CA	72
A New Era	75
Draft Picks / A New Direction	76
2018 Draft	78
Russell Wilson and Bronco's Front Office Moves	84
LET'S RIDE	89
Sean Payton / Hope for the Future	93
What Now?	100
New Era, New Hope and a Path Forward	101

Chapter 1

Wild Horses - A Denver Broncos Story - Elway Through Today

This is a book about a wild / half-tamed horse. Typically, I have some sense of wonder or would usually consider myself the type of person that really wants to learn more about the why or the what or the who... but I find it somewhat intriguing the actual definition of a Bronco is a wild or (half-tamed) horse. It was always thee team I rooted for and I knew it was associated with a horse of some kind. I just never gave it much thought. When I was really young, the thought was; they are clearly a football team and they are also a cool SUV. (We had a super sweet Black and Yellow Bronco SUV when I was young). But, Broncos actually are beautiful creatures that run free and run wild out in the western United States. This isn't really a book about how tamed a horse may, or may not, be. It is about the Denver Broncos, the NFL Football Team: the glorious franchise from the Mile High City. A Mile up there is really high - 1,760 yards above sea level. Many Founding Fathers didn't know this until George Washington provided more info regarding it. I had to speak of it in yardage for obvious reasons.

This ride (horse reference) will focus, mostly, on the 80's (Elway era) through today. - Per the last few years - and now in 2025 - I can't speak of an era in the modern age for this team. The Broncos currently don't have an identity. So, there is no era I can reference, other than stating it is through the present.

I grew up in one of the Dakotas. Once I left the state, I was surprised to realize no one cared or would even ask which Dakota. They were almost shocked that there were 2 Dakotas. Beforehand, I thought we were kind of special. But, no other human beings from other states thought I needed to distinguish... I came from the one closer to Canada. Anyway, the reason I state that: I had free rein (Broncos or horse reference) to make my selection of NFL teams. I was a HUUUUGE Footballl fan growing up in the 80's. My Mom took pictures of

Wild Horses: A Denver Broncos Story

me watching the Broncos with an Elway #7 Hutch Jersey on when I was just a tyke. In our youth, we all made a selection; the Broncos were my team! I think the main reason it started was I really liked the color - blaze orange. (You have gotta start somewhere right?) But, it evolved into something that would change my life.

Choosing the Broncos, where I came from - this was strange to most, as going down the street, 90% of the population in my hometown were Vikings fans (lived in northeastern ND, very close to the MN border). In fact, out of the approximately 1,500 people in my small town, I didn't know one other person that liked the Broncos. So, I was the smartest decision maker...and I guess I am also saying they all made dumb selections when it came to picking their favorite NFL team.

A group of us would go out to Shorty's lot and play football in our full gear and as I intimated: most were wearing a #81 Vikings Anthony Carter jersey or a #9 Tommy Kramer jersey - AKA 2 minute Tommy - that is a reference to his football prowess, and thankfully not something else (that was a mature audience joke).

Those outdoor football days/playing 4 on 4 with friends in full gear...those really were the glory days. I played High School Football and was recruited by College teams that could barely afford uniforms, and were the opposite of the cream of the crop (meaning no scholarship options and no hope of having a winning record). - These were probably the equivalent of Division 4 teams? That is the type of College who recruited me to play...anyway, you can see, I didn't have Football in my future beyond high school. In fact, beyond that, I haven't played any type of competitive or outdoor football with one exception. One night my friends and I, in our early to mid 30's, went out on a nearby street in 5 below weather during Winter, in North Dakota (pretty darn intoxicated), and threw a Tupperware container around using it as a Football. I am pretty sure we won. Pretty sure anyway. We nearly died of frostbite. But, regardless, this shows how much we all loved playing the game.

Back to us, in the 80's and 90's, when we were young: those were greatest days for me and my friends. I am going to focus on many glorious days for the Broncos franchise; and as usual, per any story out there...some not so glorious.

Chapter 2

New Franchise and a Jump to the 1980s

This is an informative and hilarious take on the Broncos franchise and it will overwhelmingly be a look at the 80's and beyond. John Elway is the guy / the Icon in franchise history...so, the look at the team is heavily influenced by his tenure and the years thereafter. I did want to give a small introduction as to how the franchise got started. Starting an NFL franchise is kind of a big deal. - Burgundy Quote

The Establishment of the Denver Broncos

The Broncos were barely competitive during their 10-year run in the AFL and their first three years in the NFL. They got their start in the AFL in 1960 and joined the NFL in 1970 as part of the merger. They didn't have a winning season until 1973 and didn't qualify for the playoffs until 1977. So, per their early years...I am going to zoom right by them because there isn't much to go over. Craig Morton was a pretty good quarterback for a time period and the Broncos were pretty mediocre overall. Let's journey to a different time period.

The 1980's

The 80's were an interesting decade for a lot of reasons. The Reagan years, the War on Drugs, the rise of the cultural phenomenon MTV, the AIDS epidemic, the Fall of the Berlin Wall, a time of bad fashion and worse music... and in the NFL: the 49ers were the team to beat. The 49ers not only had a great record overall, but they also won 4 Super Bowls in the 80's. 4 Super Bowls in 1 decade - that is pretty amazing! You had to give them maximum credit. Bill Walsh, Joe Montana, Jerry Rice, etc. - They were the gold standard in the NFL that decade. But, another team was starting to put it together - the Broncos were a top 5 team (record wise) during the time period.

Dan Reeves

In the early 80's, Denver made a special coaching hire. - Dan Reeves. Reeves' first head coaching opportunity came in 1981 and it was a risk for The Broncos. At 37, Reeves was the youngest Head Coach hired in the whole league. During his 12 years with Denver, Reeves established himself as one of the top coaches in the NFL. The Broncos became a continuous playoff contender. Reeves guided the Broncos to 6 postseason appearances during his time there. He led them to several AFC West Divisional Titles and multiple AFC Championships.

So, as you can see, the 80's under Dan Reeves were some great years for Denver. To make it to the top, you usually have to face trials and tribulations and the Broncos did just that. The Broncos were a franchise that had little to moderate success previously before Reeves arrival. Coach Reeves had sparked a level of success the Broncos had never seen up to this point.

1986: The Broncos had produced some solid drafts, and that led to an amazing year in 1986. They started hot!!! 6-0, before losing to the Jets in Week 7. They finished the year 11-5 and won their 1st 2 playoff games! In their history, the Broncos had only made the Super Bowl one other time (1977) and they did not come out victorious. 9 years later, they made it happen again. Now, most fans hoped they wouldn't just be happy to make it, but they would win the whole thing. It turns out they were just happy to make it. It wasn't the greatest Super Bowl of all time. The Giants were the favorites in this one and they did what favorites tend to do. The Broncos lost in lopsided fashion, 39-20, to Phill

Simms and the New York Giants. The Giants were Super Bowl Champs that year.

Most Bronco's fans were optimistic after the showing. Why? You had a very young coach, a young up and comer at QB and you had a solid team around him and all appeared to be getting better. This is usually how it is supposed to go. Typically, you need to lose one, to then establish yourself (especially with a very young QB as the team's leader)...then you keep coming back, getting better, only to then make it happen (hopefully) shortly thereafter.

To summarize the remainder of the 1980's and the coaching tenure: Reeves led the team to three Super Bowl appearances, including Super Bowls XXI, XXII, and XXIV, ...but unfortunately, for he, and the franchise, they lost all three.

As I stated, the Broncos did have an incredible record all decade long...and they did make Super Bowls during the remainder of the 80's. But, those Super Bowls are actually tough to talk about. If you ask any Bronco's fan that is over the age of 40, they will likely just attempt to change the subject; that is a smart move! The Broncos made the Super Bowl in 1987 and 1989. The Washington Redskins Super Bowl (Year:1987 / Super Bowl XXII) - Washington shattered the hopes of all Broncos fans fairly early in this one. The only good thing about this game: it was so lopsided at halftime, that Broncos fans mostly turned off the game at that point, so we could all just jump to our own conclusions thereafter. I remember taking off my little Elway jersey fairly early, per watching this one, yelling and pouting, and calling it a season. Sad, sad performance that day. 42-10 was the final score. 42 F'n points to 10 total for Denver.

Concluding the 80's and Summarizing the Reeves Era

Only place to go is up...after that debacle, against Washington, right? I briefly noted the awful, heartbreaking Washington Super Bowl loss. Let's just say it didn't get any better. The Broncos, under Reeves and Elway, made it back to the Big One in 1989. They physically showed up to the SuperDome in New Orleans. But, I don't know if they were aware of the fact they needed to play an NFL game. They were absolutely throttled by the 49ers: 55-10. The score remains the most lopsided scoring differential in Super Bowl history. To this day, as a Broncos fan, that was the hardest one to watch for obvious reasons. The 49ers were the heavy favorites but most hoped the Broncos could find a way to win a close one in the end. They did the opposite. It was a sad day for the franchise, and, at this point, instead of that young-buck, optimism (like after that Giants Super Bowl loss), there appeared to be a dark rain cloud hanging over Mile High Stadium. They had not just lost a huge game. They had looked completely awful doing it...and that now makes not 1, not 2, not 3, but 4 Super Bowl losses overall in the franchise's history (tying them with the Minnesota Vikings as the only teams to do so at that point). The losses also, weren't getting better, they were getting worse.

The last years of the Reeves-Elway era were marked by feuding. Reeves battled many decision-makers in Denver and he also started to take on play-calling duties after ousting Elway's favorite offensive coordinator: Mike Shanahan in the early 90's. There was a rift between he and Elway. Reeves had the absolute gall to draft a Quarterback to replace John Elway in the draft - (1st round) - of the 1992 season. Dan decided to draft Tommy Maddox out of UCLA. - Wow!! - Drafting a player at the same position as a Legend: Elway, and drafting him that early - that is a bold move. As the Coach/Decision Maker, that had better work out for you. Longer story short, it did not, and the Reeves coaching era in Denver came to an end.

Chapter 3

ELWAY

The 1980's were the Dan Reeves Coaching Years and he really is a huge name in Bronco's franchise history. They not only won games under his tutelage, and didn't t squeak into the playoffs, they made (several) Super Bowls. Obviously, this was not a small feat. He was also there for the overwhelming majority of the 1980's and coached into the 90's. But, if you ask nearly any NFL or Broncos fan...the success in the 80's was due to their electric, young Quarterback - John Elway.

1983 - Big Year for Many Reasons

Before the season, the Broncos traded with the Baltimore Colts for the rights to the 1st overall pick in the Draft. There was a Quarterback playing at the University of Stanford that many NFL Teams had their eyes on. John Elway set several career records for passing attempts and completions; he also received unanimous All-American honors while in College. Elway was the 1st overall selection in the '83 draft and the Broncos were absolutely thrilled to get him. At this point in history, this was the greatest QB draft of all time.

Quick note on this draft: 6 Quarterbacks: John Elway, Todd Blackledge, Jim Kelly, Tony Eason, Ken O'Brien, and Dan Marino were all drafted in the 1st round of this draft. That was the highest number of QBs ever taken in the 1st round (now tied for 1st). Of these quarterbacks, Elway, Kelly, Eason, and Marino played in the Super Bowl at least once. Elway, Kelly, O'Brien, and Marino were selected to play in at least 1 Pro Bowl and Elway, Kelly, and Marino have been inducted into the Pro Football Hall of Fame - the highest honor that can be bestowed on anyone who plays in the NFL. This was, without doubt, the greatest QB draft of all time.

Early Years and Early Success

John Elway and family were pretty high on themselves. That's a fact and this is coming from someone who loved Elway as the Broncos cornerstone. John Elway should have been going to the Colts with the #1 Pick. But, after consultations with his Dad and others, Elway stated he would not play for the Colts and their Coach Frank Kush. Kush was noted as a tough Disciplinarian (kind of an A-Hole) and Elway and family didn't feel they would mesh well together. So, Elway threatened, if drafted by the Colts, to go play Major League Baseball and spurn the NFL entirely. The teams worked out a deal and Elway ended up moving to the Mile High City to play for Denver.

Previous to Elway arriving, Craig Morten had some decent seasons as the Denver QB. But, Elway looked to be a different type of player / different type of arm / a different type of athlete overall. But, like it is for most, all doesn't usually start off perfectly. As a Rookie Quarterback in the NFL, you are extremely likely to run into many bumps in the road. This proved true for Elway in his first season. Elway was named the starting QB in his first ever professional game. But, those good tidings didn't last long. He was replaced by veteran Steve Deberg due to a poor performance. This continued to happen (poor performances), until one day, Coach Reeves said, Elway isn't ready and he went to Deberg on a full-time basis. Regardless, the vibes in Denver were extremely positive. 1983 was a good year for several reasons. They had a solid win-loss (9-7) record, they made the playoffs, and their draft turned out multiple big-time players. The Broncos appeared to be building something that was headed in the right direction.

1984: My favorite book is 1984 by George Orwell. Orwell's 1984 is not a happy story. Flip-Side - 1984 was a darn good year for the Broncos. They were led by 2nd year signal caller: John Elway. He was given the reins (horse reference) to be their QB the whole season. Elway didn't have an amazing first year in the Orange and Blue. But, his 2nd year was pretty darn good. He was still a very young QB getting to know the team, the playbook, the NFL, etc. - so, to guide the team to a 13-3 regular season record, while making the playoffs... that is exactly what you want to see. They did not win a playoff game that year. But, as was just mentioned, they were building things properly and were heading in the right direction. 1985 was another great year. They didn't make the playoffs due to odd performances from some other teams, but it was yet another stepping stone in the right direction.

In 1986, the Broncos put it all together. The team, led by Elway, had another great season. Per Wins and Losses, they were near the top of the league. That season, Elway led the Broncos to Super Bowl XXI, after defeating the Cleveland Browns, in the AFC Championship, on a famous possession at the end of the fourth quarter that became known as "The Drive." The Drive: In a span of 5 minutes and a few seconds, Elway led his team 98 yards to tie the game with 37 seconds left in regulation. The Broncos won the game in overtime. Wow...onto the Super Bowl!

Thereafter, Elway and the Broncos started out the Super Bowl against the Giants well, building a 10–7 lead and then driving to the Giants 1-yard line in the second quarter. However, the Broncos lost five yards on their next three plays and came up empty after their Kicker Rich Karlis missed an easy field goal attempt. From that point on, the rest of the game went downhill for the Broncos. Elway was sacked in the end zone for a safety on the Broncos ensuing possession, cutting their lead to 10–9. Then in the second half, it was an absolute disaster. The Giants scored 30 points and ended up winning the game 39–20. Still, glass half full: Elway had an impressive performance, throwing for 304 yards, and a touchdown, while also leading Denver in rushing with 27 yards and a touchdown on the ground.

Per Elway, and the Broncos, this was what all fans were looking for. There was a massive amount of hope. They were, without doubt, headed in the right direction and this was the start of it all. The next few years: Elway and the squad made it to the big game, but they did not perform well and that is an understatement. The rest of the '80s were highlighted by regular season wins and enormous Super Bowl losses (some of the biggest differentials ever seen in the NFL) - in Bronco's Super Bowl losses to both the Redskins and the 49ers. At the end of the decade, all Bronco's fans were happy they were making it; but, obviously, there was a feeling of being unsettled. Let us jump to what I consider to be the best decade. (for multiple reasons)

The 90's

We move into a new decade: the 90's. The Rise of the Internet, Rise of Personal Computers, The Clinton Years, The Jordan Years, Gangster Rap and the (further) Rise of Hip Hop, Grunge Rock, etc. etc. - Helluva 10 year span. Quick tidbit on their most recent "performance" - The '89 season and the way it ended was seemingly a jolt to the franchise (and not in a good way). There is losing and there is getting downright embarrassed. This was the latter. We have all heard the phrase: "get over it." Per that Super Bowl loss, the Broncos apparently could not. In 1990 and the ensuing years, the Broncos were bad, if not awful. There is no getting around it. Their Super Bowl hangover lasted for years. This was a team, in the 80's, that had become used to winning, not just barely making it happen, but winning a high percentage of their games and making it to the big one.

That changed - that 49ers Super Bowl loss hit the team hard. They couldn't figure out how to return from it. The 1991 season was one of the worst in franchise history. 1992 was better and they made the playoffs...only to lose to the Buffalo Bills. But no one thought they had much of a shot that year. The 49ers took something from Denver and there was concern they were ever going to get it back.

1992 was also worth (re) mentioning as Dan Reeves thought it was time to replace their Franchise Quarterback: Elway, with another young gun from the West Coast-Tommy Maddox, from UCLA. Reeves and Elway: their relationship clearly soured. Reeves was sent packing and the Broncos moved the ship forward, with Elway as the undisputed captain.

Chapter 4

Mike Shanahan and Terrell Davis

Dan Reeves was shown the door and John Elway was still the guy at Quarterback for the Mile High City Franchise. The Broncos used (wasted) their 1st round pick on an eventual replacement for QB (Maddox). As I have already mentioned, this didn't work; it was a bad pick, and most already thought they had their guy (in Elway). The early 90's through the mid-90's were fairly successful for Denver. But, most thought of Denver as the "can't quite get over the hump" franchise and rightfully so - they had been a professional football franchise for over 35 years and didn't have 1 championship to show for it.

Wade Phillips was hired to take over for Dan Reeves in Denver and coached the Broncos for 2 pretty forgettable seasons. Phillip's tenure with

Denver can be described as mediocre. Phillips had been the Defensive Coordinator for several previous seasons and most thought he could possibly chart a new course for the franchise. He could not make that happen. After watching Phillips as the Head Coach for a fairly short amount of time, most thought Wade was a nice, lovable guy, but they didn't think he could lead an NFL team in the right direction. Phillips was fired after the 1994 season...compiling a record of 16-16. Defining average.

1995: This was the Broncos 36th professional football season overall. The season would be a turning point for the franchise. This would be the first year, for their newly hired Head Coach: Mike Shanahan. Mike Shanahan had a previous stint with the Los Angeles Raiders as Head Coach in the late 80's. This did not go well and it did not last long. He was fired during his 2nd season there. Due to that move by the Raiders eccentric owner: Al Davis - most wondered if Shanahan was even head coaching material. The Broncos certainly thought he was and they were happy to give him a shot. This was a Franchise-Altering moment for the Denver Broncos.

In 1995, the Broncos brought in what they felt was an offensive guru in Mike Shanahan. They felt, with his innovative offensive strategies and his ability to develop quarterbacks -this would make him the guy. This proved to be great forethought; this is one of the few marriages that actually worked out for quite a long time. Shanahan is known for his West Coast, one-cut and go running style, and play action passes. But, like any coach, he would need the right combination on offense. They had the right QB, a nice Wide Receiving corps, Good Tight Ends, and their line was fairly solid. But, who knew what the plan was for the 1995 NFL Draft? The 1995 NFL Draft was an interesting one in that the 1st pick overall was a massive bust (Ki-Jana Carter). But, there were many great game-changing players drafted thereafter. Tony Boselli, the late Steve McNair, Kerry Collins, and Warren Sapp to name a few. But these were all 1st round picks. The Broncos did not not have an early round pick (not even close). They didn't have a pick until the 4th round overall. But, a barely thought of 6th round pick would prove to be the steal of the draft. In the 6th round , at the 196th pick overall, the Broncos selected Terrell Davis: Running Back out of Georgia. When you draft in the 6th or 7th rounds, you cross your fingers and hope for a miracle. The Broncos wish was granted.

Terrell Davis

Terrell Davis was brought in to see if he could make the team. Most thought he would not. As was stated, if you are picked that late in the draft, no one expects much from you. In fact, most hope you will come in and be an impact player on Special Teams. Terrell Davis knew that and he made an impact right out of the gates. I have watched football since I was a little guy in the 80's; the only play I will never forget from a pre-season NFL game on Special Teams - Terrell Davis made a tackle on a 49ers player and the stadium erupted...as it was so noticeable, and such a massive hit. After that play, Shanahan, the coaching staff, everyone noticed. They thought the Georgia product could certainly make a name for himself on Special Teams...but what about anywhere else?

Special Teams is the most boring unit on an NFL team. It is important. But, the cream of the crop units - Offense and Defense - that is where a player wants to be. Terrell Davis was drafted as a Running Back. He was given a shot at a few carries for the Broncos on offense. He was good, so good, you couldn't help but give him more carries. Longer story short - Terrell took leadership of the #1 Running Back position and never looked back. That year, his rookie year: Davis had nearly 1,500 yards from scrimmage and 8 total touchdowns. - Not bad for a Rookie, and a 6th round pick, who was slated to either be on special teams or not make the team at all. The Broncos team, as a whole, also had a decent year. They were not great...they dealt with injuries and poor performances in big moments, and they went 8-8. They missed the playoffs that year. But, they seemed like they were really putting the pieces in place. They now had young up and coming Wide Receivers: Rod Smith and Ed McCaffrey. Shannon Sharpe was one of the best Tight Ends in the league, and Terrell Davis looked to be something special overall at the Running Back position. Combining them with John Elway and Mike Shanahan, they might have something here.

1996

This was a special year for many reasons. They took that 8-8 record and they improved on it in an incredible way. The Broncos pieces seemed to be in place; this was a year that looked very promising. This was the year they clinched the AFC West for the 1st time since 1991. Early out of the gates (horse reference) - they went 12-1 in their first 13 games. They were the perfect combination of passing/running. Their final regular season record: 13-3 was tied for the best record in the entire league. They easily made the playoffs and would have a 1st round bye. They would also be in what looked to be a great position.

Start of the playoffs: They were playing against a Jacksonville Jaguars team that was a recent expansion team. It is almost unheard for a new expansion team to have any early success for several years. This was a strange situation; Jacksonville made the playoffs in their 2nd year overall (as a Franchise in the NFL). This was the perfect recipe for the Broncos however; The Broncos should be able to get an easy victory. Thereafter, they would head to the AFC Championship and then go after that elusive first Super Bowl! Quick note: The Broncos had been a professional franchise since 1960 and the Jaguars had only been around for less than 2 years. This should have been easy pickings for the Broncos.

Unfortunately, the Jaguars had other plans. This game was going as it should be early. The Broncos were up 12-0 in the 2nd quarter and they looked to be on their way to a lopsided victory. As I stated, it didn't quite turn out that way. The 1980's Super Bowl losses were hard. They were really hard...not so much the 39-20 loss to the Giants - that was a young team, young QB (Elway), and they were trying to find their way, and they appeared to be happy to just make the Super Bowl. But, the last 2

Super Bowl losses were more challenging. (losses to Washington and San Francisco: they were not favored in either game and most experts thought they would lose. They did...but still tough on the team and fanbase to get destroyed like that).

But, the loss to the Jaguars was like a punch to the gut, a really hard one to take. This was the best Broncos team I had ever seen; this was their best shot. They had the proven Pro-bowl QB and a guy who was in the MVP discussion: Elway. They had the offensive genius: Shanahan leading the team, talent everywhere on the field, etc, etc. They were playing against a team that was just happy to even be in the playoffs and they lose???!??!??! Tough. To. Take.

There was now no doubt about it. The Broncos were now in SAD franchise territory. John Elway had now been in the league for over 12 years, and the franchise still had not won the big one. Frankly, after so many 1980's Super Bowl losses, they were probably already there. But, without doubt, per NFL Standards, they were right up at the top of the shit-heap... with the Vikings and the Bills. These were the NFL teams that ALWAYS found a way to lose when it matters most. These were the 3 franchises that had lost 4 Super Bowls and had never won, not once and had been around for decades! Now, at this point, losing sounded inevitable. It wasn't a matter of if, but when. There **should** be hope in this squad as they retained the overwhelming majority of their talent going in to next season. But, after seeing so many losses at the wrong time, from teams led by John Elway, should any of us expect to see anything different?

Chapter 5

Late 20th Century Broncos Football

Now, the Broncos, AKA the little Donkeys, were going into their 38th professional season. Yeah, I said little Donkeys. I am very mad at this franchise at the start of the 1997 season. They have lost their title as beautiful, majestic semi-tamed horses. They were now something different. Was there hope for this season? I don't know. Probably not. But, they will still play it out and see what happens.

A sad part of this story is John Elway. Keep in mind - he is no foal (horse reference) anymore. He was drafted in 1983. By 1997, and by the standards of the NFL in the 80's and 90's, Elway was wearing down. He had to be. Quarterbacks in 80s and 90s actually got hit by Defenders. When the contact happened, a QB didn't just get hugged and placed on the ground lightly, so a defender wouldn't get called for a personal foul. (today's standards) They were violently pile-driven into the ground over and over again and the refs barely batted an eye. It is not like now with Patrick Mahomes playing...where if someone breaths on him the wrong way, that defender is suspended for the season. Lucky over-commercialized Prick! Sorry, blacked out for a second talking about Mahomes...Digressing.

Back to 1997: 1997 was a hell of a season. The Broncs started 6-0 and were 9-1 after their first 10 games. After a 9-1 start, fans were starting to get an optimistic feeling that this was THE YEAR. The shit feelings from the year prior were in the rearview mirror. After starting 11-2, they hit some bumps in the road, the last few weeks of the regular season. They still made the playoffs but losing 2 out of your last 3 games in the regular season...that is not really the momentum you are looking for going into the biggest games of the year. Elway probably had 1 of his best statistical years of all time in 1997. But, that did not and could not overshadow the fact that the window was closing. Quarterbacks nearing 40 years old don't usually last a whole lot longer. It was a proven fact. The Broncos had very little room for error going into these playoffs.

1997 Playoffs

The 1st round of the 1997 Playoffs was the biggest game in the modern history of the franchise. They, due to stumbling at the end of the regular season, had to play in the 1st round (no bye week gifted). This would make the road harder overall. But, hey, you made your bed, now you must lie in it. Also, they had quite a history with their opponent. They actually lost to this opponent in dramatic (and sad) fashion the year prior:. They were taking on the Jacksonville Jaguars and this was the ultimate revenge game. Going into this game, I was at a divergent road: I was anticipating good things, but also anticipating what I thought was the inevitable...them making a mess of things as they always do at some point in the playoffs. Now, playing the Jaguars (again in the playoffs)...I was the epitome of nervous.

The Broncos started the scoring early and were looking good after Quarter 1 - they were up 14-0. To say I was excited, this would be a large understatement. But keep in mind, they were up big the year prior, after the 1st quarter, to the same team, and they lost. So, I am still worried. That ended up making a lot of sense. After 3 quarters, I was of course nearing the edge of a cliff. The score was 21-17 going into the 4th Quarter. They couldn't lose this one right? There was no way the Broncos could pull it off again could they?!!???? - Meaning find a way to lose when it mattered the most? No. They wouldn't do that. Not this time.

The Broncos were incredible in the 4th Quarter against Jacksonville. Game total: Denver compiled 310 rushing yards and 511 total yards of offense, and held the ball for 41 minutes (out of 60) in a 42–17 win, avenging their playoff loss to the Jaguars the year before. They absolutely crushed the Jags in the 4th Quarter. A combination of timely passing, great rushing plays, and amazing interceptions, and sacks by the Defense...the Broncos advanced to play in the next round!

I was thrilled but still skeptical. As I stated, they made it harder on themselves by not getting any bye weeks. So, they needed to play the hated Chiefs in the Divisional round in Kansas City. K.C. was the #1 seed in the AFC. Kansas City is also known as one of the, if not the, hardest stadiums to play in. So, most experts gave KC the upper-hand. Most experts appeared to be right; it looked grim until the 4th quarter. Elway then hit Easy Ed McCaffrey for a 43 yard bomb, then Terrell Davis scored, what turned out to be, the game wining Touchdown. WHEW!

AFC Title Game

Wild Horses: A Denver Broncos Story

The Steelers: they are seemingly always good. You don't want to play in Pittsburgh. But, you really don't want to play them in Pittsburgh, in January, in the AFC Championship. This was going to be really, really hard. (that's what she said - sorry, had to be done)

Back to it - the 1st half was filled with quite a bit of scoring...more than most thought. But, the Broncos held an advantage and it was looking good. Then the 4th quarter hit; the Broncos still had a nice lead. But, Kordell Stewart and the Steelers scored with around 3 minutes left to go. It was now much too close and it was getting downright scary. 3 minutes left in the game...the time couldn't go quickly enough. The Broncos made big plays when they counted the most. Elway, Shannon Sharpe, and Ed McCaffrey all made big plays to make sure this was a Broncos VICTORY! They had made it back! Now, on to the biggest game in Broncos franchise HISTORY!

Super Bowl : Green Bay Packers vs. Denver Broncos 1997 Season, Date: January 25th, 1998

I was born in the early 80's. I had only witnessed the Broncos losing every big game they had ever played. This Super Bowl against Green Bay: I had anticipated this game like a 6 year old waiting for Santa Claus to arrive on Christmas Day. There were

2 weeks in between the AFC Championship and the Super Bowl. I don't know how I made it; it was much too long a duration. There is a team in the NFL I love. There are teams I like. There are teams that I don't like and there are teams that I hate with every fiber of my being. - The Green Bay Packers - they were that team.

I hated their team colors, I didn't like the state of Wisconsin and their incessant cheese references, and they were a huge rival to Minnesota (whom I have close ties with). I didn't like the constant love given to one guy over and over and over again: Brett Favre. In 1998, Brett Favre walked on water and every announcer would let you know that every time he stepped on the field. If he threw an interception, it was always someone else's fault. This awe-shucks, Mississippi Hillbilly, was seemingly everyone's favorite, and everyone was excited to see he, (the league MVP) and the Packers perform.

The Packers were the heavy favorite in this game as well. Frankly, before this game started, I was excited but my excitement was outweighed by sheer nervousness. I was actually scared. This was not a feeling you want going in to watch a Super Bowl. Keep in mind: I had watched the 3 previous Super Bowls in the 80's. They weren't just losses. They were embarrassments. These games were not only embarrassing to John Elway and Denver. It was embarrassing to the NFL. If the Broncos decided to lose the Super Bowl again, by over 30 points, I was worried the NFL might just kick Denver out of the league.

The wait is over; it is a beautiful Sunday in sunny San Diego. I was invited to Super Bowl parties that day. I declined. It might sound strange but I needed to watch this one on my own. If I was going to blow a gasket...I wanted it to be by myself.

The start of the game / the kickoff: My reason for being extremely nervous appeared to rear its ugly head: the Packers took the kickoff and moved down the field with little to no resistance. Early, VERY early in this one - the score was already 7-0, Packers, and I was starting to have awful flashbacks to past Super Bowl performances.

But, to my surprise, and possibly to the surprise, of many scorned Broncos fans...they decided to fight back. And, it actually started looking good - really good. Am I in a dream? Are the Broncos performing well in the biggest of big games? Do they actually have a shot against the vaunted, highly favored Green Bay Packers? Soon, instead of being nervous about this one being a blow-out, I actually had thoughts Denver might win the game.

The Broncos converted two turnovers to take a 17–7 lead in the second quarter before the Packers cut the score to 17–14 at halftime. I felt great (obviously) at halftime and was really starting to believe. Jumping to the last quarter: 24 - 17 in the 4th Quarter - Denver was still up. I couldn't contain myself. This was going to happen, right??!??!?!

That was a fleeting feeling. In the 4th, Green Bay drove down the field...they tied the game. I automatically revert to negative thoughts and think it is all downhill from here. The favorite, Green Bay Packers, are going to keep their momentum going and Denver will do what they always do in these situations - fold. But, something strange happened that day. Denver did not fold.

Both Defenses made some stops. Then, something magical happened. My favorite player in the league: running back Terrell Davis, scored a touchdown with under 2 minutes left to go!!!!!! The Broncos were now up! Green Bay made many plays on their final drive and I kept thinking the worst, kept thinking the other shoe would drop...but it never happened. Final seconds ticked on the clock and the horn sounded...

CHAMPS - The Top of the Mountain!

The Denver Broncos were the Super BOWL CHAMPS!!!!!!!!!!!!! - Final Score: 31-24. I felt elation like I had never felt before. I was a 16 year old Junior in High School. I hadn't felt much at that point in my life frankly...but this feeling was incredible. I liked multiple sports. But, football trumped them all. I liked many teams, but the Broncos trumped all others. This felt like a dream. Given other franchises, and their circumstances, this was not the biggest obstacle overcome by a team. But, keep in mind - as a Broncos fan growing up in the 80's, I watched the worst performances in Super Bowls ever. I thought Elway would retire, never to win the biggest of big games. This just happened. They had reached the top of the mountain!

Clearly, I was on cloud 9 due to the Broncos incredible performance. These were 37 years of not winning as a professional football organization. Then, one day, after all of the losses, headaches and disappointments, they win it - the ultimate game - the Super Bowl! Despite suffering a migraine headache that caused him to miss most of the second quarter, Davis was named the Super Bowl MVP -he ran for 157 yards, combined for nearly 170 total, and scored a Super Bowl record - three rushing touchdowns. As of 2024, Davis remains the most recent running back to be named Super Bowl MVP. If you are a sports fan and especially, if you are an NFL fan, you know: this was the greatest day ever!

Chapter 6

1998 and Saying Goodbye

Coming off of the biggest high I had ever experienced…I was living the dream and felt a level of euphoria I had never felt. I know many other Bronco's fans shared that exact sentiment as well. This was a big deal for so many reasons…

Elway - At this point, many thought he would call it a career. He was nearing 40 years old. In the NFL, that is a super senior citizen. He had taken many hits and had many injuries. His body was breaking down and he had just finally won that elusive Super Bowl trophy. After 15 seasons in the NFL, he could now call it a day and no one would judge him for it. No one would say, well this guy is pretty good, but he just could not win the big one. He had finally done it, and he was in a position to retire on top and ride off (horse reference) into the sunset. The

Broncos had been at it professionally for nearly 40 years total and now they can finally say they are Super Bowl Champions! Combining all those numbers, no one would have batted an eye if Elway called it quits. All was right with the world. But, for most athletes, once you taste that sweet victory cigar, you want more.

So, the Broncos ran it back the next year. The Broncos weren't just adequate that season; they were better than ever. There was not only a Super Bowl in their cross-hairs, but a perfect season looked to be a possibility.

Start of the 1998 season: All were just happy to see them bring the majority of the team back. Obviously, we were all thrilled for them to make (what could be) one last run at a title with John Elway leading the pack. They started the season by beating the Patriots in a fairly close game 27-21. But, the next few games: the Broncos were annihilating their opposition. Games were not even close. They were winning games by 20 and 30 points, week after week. The NFL is usually quite competitive. These were extreme differentials; the Broncos were just that good. The regular season starts in early September. It was now early December and the Broncos were still undefeated! They had just beat the hated division rival Kansas

City Chiefs; they were now 13-0 and were on a quest for an undefeated season. By now in December, most NFL teams, no matter how good they are, have a hiccup or two, of sorts. Injuries, combined with a random turnover, or just flat out bad luck... typically you will have lost a game or two or three...as I stated, even if you're a great team. But, this was special; this was an incredible year. The Broncos were a dominant 13-0 and they were looking to challenge the '72 Dolphins. - The Dolphins were the only team to run the table and go undefeated in the regular season and win the Super Bowl.

Fans and players alike were having a blast! This was even better than the year prior when they won the whole damn thing. The next week: game 14 of the season...all came crashing down. They played in NY against the Giants and they just didn't quite have it. They seemed to be going through the motions and they lost a close game. Giants 20 Broncos 16. The '72 Dolphins were all popping champagne; their players loved being the only team in history to go undefeated (and rightfully so). Obviously, all was not lost. The Broncos were still 13-1 and still in great position to do what every team sets out to do when they start the year - win the Super Bowl.

The next game: another tough loss. Most would agree they played their worst game in quite a while in losing to the Dolphins. These losses could no longer be considered an aberration; this looked to be a possible trend. Instead of vying for perfection, most fans were now worried about them carrying some kind of good vibes / momentum into the playoffs. The next week came; this was the last tune-up before the playoffs started. This was now a huge game! And...whew...nice times: They put it together and beat the Seahawks to end the season at 14-2. That was a big deal. This was still a great year. They are now going into the playoffs and they are back to their winning ways. They also get a bye week to rest up. This was big for many in the organization and was huge to a guy like John Elway who was now in his 16th NFL Season.

Playoffs - 1998

They played that same Miami Dolphins team during the divisional round of the playoffs. The Broncs were feeling refreshed after watching the rest of the playoffs that first weekend. It showed. They avenged their late regular season loss and they destroyed the Dolphins at home in Mile High: 38-3, in their first playoff game. This game was not close; the Broncos took care of business and it was never in doubt. Fans were now feeling pretty great again.

This looked like the team that ripped 13 victories in a row to start the regular season.

They next played against the NY Jets in the AFC Title Game. NY teams have not been kind to them recently as they lost their undefeated season to the Giants just a few weeks back. This was a bit tighter; but not real close...the Broncos pulled away and took out the Jets in a Mile High home game. WHOO! They were on their way back to the Super Bowl! This was my favorite NFL year in the history of the NFL. The '98 season - This season only barely squeaks by the previous Super Bowl victory year for Denver. Why? I loved the Broncos and also was a Vikings Fan.

I had grown up on the border of MN/ND. Most of my friends were Vikings fans and my whole family rooted on the Purple and Gold. So, nearing this AFC/NFC Championship weekend, the trash talk was continuous and the excitement was palpable. Bets were already placed on who would win: the Broncos or the Vikings.

This was to be the matchup of the 2 best teams in the league. All experts assumed with about 99% certainty the Super Bowl would be between Minnesota and Denver. Randall Cunningham/ Randy Moss and company were leading MN to the promised land for the first time in their franchise's history. The Broncos had an amazing regular season; they went 14-2. But, the Vikings actually had the best record in the league: 15-1, and had a historic season. The Vikings broke records on offense; they would actually be the favored team when the 2 teams would inevitably match up in the Super Bowl! This would be a match-up of 2 juggernauts; these were 2 amazing teams and they were destined to play each other. For me, and friends and family, it was the perfect combination and it would be the most fun sporting event of our lifetimes.

The Championship games were played and the weekend came to an end. Sadly: the Vikings didn't hold up their end of the bargain. They were playing against a huge underdog in Minneapolis, in their home stadium: the Metrodome, and they lost to the Atlanta Falcons. Being a massive Broncos fan, when the weekend came to an end, I couldn't be that saddened by the overall turn of events. But, I felt bad for those closest to me and Minnesota as they had been in the NFL for nearly 40 years and had Zero Super Bowl wins...but, you have to move on, in football, and in life. I was given another chance to watch the Broncos and John Elway in the Super Bowl!

Super Bowl XXXIII January 31st, 1999

I was soon going to be graduating from High School (in May of that year anyway). My life was going to be very different in a few months. I spurned all invitations for Super Bowl get-togethers as I wanted full attention on this game. The Falcons were big underdogs in this matchup. But, the Falcons were big underdogs against the Vikings and they pulled it off in Minnesota at the Vikings home stadium. I was worried it could happen again. It was the Mile High Salute vs. the Dirty Birds. The Broncos were facing the Falcons, who were led by Dan Reeves. - Yes, that same Dan Reeves. This was a massive game for many reasons. On to it... The Game / the Super Bowl: this one wasn't really all that close. I was used to close games or Bronco's extreme defeats. It was great to be on the other side of the spectrum.

Aided by John Elway's 80 yard touchdown bomb to Wide Receiver: Rod Smith, the Broncos scored 17 consecutive points to build a 17–3 lead in the second quarter from which Atlanta could not recover. The Broncos won the game; they were again the best in the league - they were Super Bowl Champions - back to back!!!!! I was, once again, on cloud nine living the Frigging DREAM!

It wasn't all elation and a reason to cheer thereafter though. Don't get me wrong; it was as great of a feeling as the year prior when they beat Green Bay and hoisted their first EVER Super Bowl Trophy. But, there was a big decision to be made about the future of the franchise.

Retirement / Last Ride

Elway announced his retirement on May 2, 1999. That Super Bowl against Atlanta: Elway completed 18 of 29 passes for 336 yards with one touchdown, and also scored a 3-yard rushing touchdown. At 38 years old / at that point in the NFL's history, Elway became the oldest player to be named Super Bowl MVP! Wow. There is no more appropriate way for a player, who is noted as one of the greatest of all time at his position, to ride off into the sunset. The Franchise player; the go-to, for the team for nearly 2 decades called it a day. Elway / The Broncos were now one of the greatest teams in the history of the league and you can argue they were the team of the decade in the 1990's (much like San Francisco in the 80's and the Steelers from the 70's). Cowboy's fans might complain about that moniker being handed to Denver; but they complain about everything, so who cares.

You can debate many topics in sports. But, when it comes to the Denver Broncos, there is one thing you cannot debate: John Elway is the greatest player in franchise history and his name is synonymous with the Denver Broncos. When you mention Denver in the sports name-game challenge, people say his name automatically, and rightfully so. His retirement left the team with a hole as big as the Grand Canyon. (that is near Denver)

Chapter 7

Moving into the New Millennium

When speaking of the Denver Broncos moving to the 1999/2000 season and beyond, the biggest story (and it wasn't even close) - was who would be the new leader of the herd? (Wild Horses reference). They did have a plan. I guess? Previously, only a couple of years back: the Broncos selected Brian Griese: QB - Michigan, in the 3rd round, the 91st pick overall. Brian was given extra credit as his Dad was multi-time Super Bowl winning Quarterback Bob Griese. After watching John Elway play some of the best football of his career, fans were expecting more great things. Broncos fans were now becoming used to watching a great team compete at the highest of levels. This was their opportunity to win 3 straight Super Bowl Championships. When you win 3 straight, you are now considered a Dynasty. That is the ultimate indicator of success for an NFL franchise.

This would continue, right? Great play overall / wins, and upper-level play? The answer, unfortunately, is no. When John Elway retired, the Broncos had more than a little trouble adapting and moving forward. In 1999, Griese became the Broncos' starting quarterback. Griese had a poor passer rating his first season as starter (2nd year overall). Things weren't looking good with him, and in turn, weren't looking good with the team. That first year, A.E. - After Elway - the Broncos were no longer riding high - At this point, you get it, I am no longer going to reference my horse / broncos references in parentheses. The Broncos went 6-10. Ugh. This was a tough pill to swallow. We all had hopes that they could possibly challenge for a 3rd Super Bowl in a ROW!! Not even close.

In the early 2000's, Brian Griese could be described as adequate. In 2000, he had a pretty darn good year and so did Denver. They had a good year, not special, but good. They made the playoffs that year but lost in the 1st round to the Ravens. For a franchise used to making it the AFC Championship or the Super Bowl, this was not exactly what we were looking for. But, there was some positive momentum. The Broncos drafted well for a few years and they were looking to mix young players with some established veterans and make a run at the Super Bowl. In 2001, those hopes were unfulfilled.

Terrell Davis Legacy

In 2001, the Bronco's year was the epitome of mediocre. They still had some of the most amazing players the franchise had ever seen. But, they were aging and getting injured at higher clip. After the 1998 season, Terrell Davis was plagued with injuries and saw less and less action. In 1999, Davis tore his ACL and MCL while trying to make a tackle in a game vs the Jets, during the fourth game of the season. That injury took him out for the entire year. In 2000, and 2001, and beyond...injuries also plagued Davis, forcing him to make a decision.

Davis decided to retire in 2002. He walked through the tunnel in uniform for the final time during a preseason Denver - San Francisco matchup, held at Mile High. To a standing ovation, Davis gave a mile-high salute to the fans and was hugged by his teammates. The Elway retirement was sad in 1999 (very sad). For me, the T.D. retirement might have been sadder. Davis only played a few seasons in the NFL. I feel he could have been one of the greatest Running Backs of all time, had he only been given more years on the field. But, we will never know.

Per the franchise overall, this would be a challenge...a big one. You have not only lost the leader of your team in Elway. This is the toughest position to fill in sports: QB. Shortly thereafter...you are now without your most dynamic player on offense (T. Davis), and one of the greatest running backs (when healthy) the league has ever seen. This usually affects you in a very negative way; this was the case with the early 2000's Denver Broncos.

That Didn't Last Long

Griese had one decent year and several poor years with Denver. He was a slow footed, weak armed, fairly cerebral Quarterback. He was decent but really was nothing special. This was not all his fault. Trent Dilfer, recently won a Super Bowl, with the Baltimore Ravens. He was not an elite Quarterback. But, he and the team found a way to win the whole thing. Truth be told: that reason was their defense - the Ravens, in the early 2000s, were historically good.

But, Griese: he was replacing a legend. And, in terms of Denver, he was trying to replace thee legend, the Franchise. Due to his mediocre performances and his penchant for turning the ball over, the Broncos released Brian Griese before the 2003 season.

This was nothing new for an NFL franchise. It is not atypical for a team to struggle to replace one of the best ever. Denver, after getting older, and losing both Elway and Terrell Davis, they decided to go in a different direction. But, the question from that point forward is...who would they go to, and how might they find a way back to the top?

Chapter 8

New Hope with the Snake

After the departure of Brian Griese at the Quarterback position, the Broncos once again, needed to attempt to regroup and figure out who they wanted to be the leader of the squad. This would not be easy. As they have seen, Quarterbacks don't just fall in your laps. This was the most challenging position to fill and they needed to do something. Enter: Jake Plummer. Not everyone was thrilled with this move. Plummer, in recent years with the Arizona Cardinals, put up similar numbers to Griese. The hope of finding that go-to legend to fill the shoes of Elway...didn't appear to be in the cards here. Jake Plummer, at least, could move around, he had some mobility, so he could gain some rushing yardage here and there. This was something the Broncos hadn't seen much of since the mid-90's. Plus he had a cool nickname: Jake the Snake. (funny note: he and Wrestling Star

Jake Roberts both took their nicknames from Kenny Stabler).

Back to Plummer's possibly play on the field - at least it was new...much like a new car, people are excited to see what it can do. We were all excited to see what the franchise could do in moving in a different direction. That year, his first year with the Broncos - Plummer and Denver made some big strides. They went 10-6 and made the playoffs! Per the actual playoffs, I will not say much. They were destroyed by Indy and Peyton Manning. But hey, they made some great progress and all were looking forward to the next year.

2004: the Broncos were not only excited to possibly build on the momentum of the year prior, but they also made a big move: they acquired Cornerback Champ Bailey in a trade with with the Washington Redskins, sending their young, up and coming superstar Running Back: Clinton Portis to Washington in return. Many were fairly saddened by the fact that they were getting rid of a Superstar RB in Portis. But, some were positively thrilled with the move...and as you saw Champ Bailey play more and more, they weren't disappointed. The season was yet another good year for the Broncos. But those pesky Colts, once again, matched up with Denver early in the playoffs...and yet again, Peyton

Manning, and those Colts, destroyed Denver. It was hard to complain though. The Broncos were playing winning football and they were making the playoffs. Let's see what they can do if they make a few adjustments.

2005: Denver was great! They had an amazing year. 13-3: regular season record. It is challenging to win that many games. This was the 1st year the fanbase had (real) hope since the end of the 1998 season. All looked as though it was coming together and the Broncos were a real threat to win it all! Denver was so good that year...they started the playoffs with a bye week. The next week: the divisional round, they took on and defeated the hated New England Patriots, led by Bill Belichick and Tom Brady. That was a HUGE Deal. At that point, in 2005, the Patriots were the best in the league. New England had just won back to back Super Bowl Championships. The heavy lifting appeared to be over... and now, all they had to do, was beat the Pittsburgh Steelers at home in Denver. The Broncos played one of the worst games they had played all year and lost to Pittsburgh. There would be no Super Bowl magic coming back to Denver.

Moving on - Denver, after nearly making the Super Bowl with Jake Plummer in 2005...would see some very lean years thereafter. In 2006, Denver made some great draft picks and they would be very helpful additions to the team. But, after a 7-2 start, Denver fizzled out and ended up 9-7. They did not make the playoffs that year. Near the end of the year, the team and Jake Plummer were starting to play poorly. That meant; the Broncos decision makers had to determine who to give the reins to for the future at QB. They decided it was time for a new era.

Jay Cutler

This era is barely worth mentioning. The Broncos became mediocre. Year, after year, they found a way to lose games and not make the playoffs. Jay Cutler was the type of Quarterback that makes the scouts swoon. He had a STRONG arm...one of the, if not the, strongest arms in the entire league. That always makes scouts and coaches say - what if? What if this guy, puts it all together, and becomes the next big thing in the league. Let's just say - Jay Cutler would not. The guy is a real A-Hole (other terms that come to mind: DBag). He didn't have close to what it takes to succeed in the NFL. But, as I said, everyone loved his "potential." The Broncos, picking up on that, decided to trade him to the Bears after only a few short, unsuccessful years with the franchise. The Bears acquired their "strong armed" quarterback filled with "potential" and the

Broncos got Kyle Orton (yawn) in return. For the Broncos, it was back to the drawing board.

New Direction / The Break-Up

2008/2009 - these years have to be mentioned...not because of any Denver Broncos success. But, they will be mentioned because of the seismic move made at the Head Coaching position. Mike Shanahan, after the 2008 NFL Season, was fired. NFL Head Coaching Spots can be akin to toys that children play with at an early age. Owners, similar to children, have their fun with them for 2 or possibly 3 years, then all parties move on. In the NFL, like it or not, that is kind of a normal scenario. For every long tenured coach like Tom Landry, Don Shula or Chuck Knoll, there are several guys named Wade Phillips, Art Shell, Cam Cameron, etc - these are guys that didn't last past 2 years with the franchise.

So, if you are thinking of it that way...it was kind of bound to happen right? Many Broncos fans, including myself, hated the move. Mike Shanahan wasn't just a good coach. He was the greatest coach in Denver Broncos history. Shanahan was an innovator on offense; he led them to their first Super Bowl victory ever and his winning percentage overall was incredible.

Shanahan posted the most wins in National Football League history during a three-year period at the time (46 in 1996–98).

Shanahan has the Highest winning percentage in Denver history (.646) and most wins in Denver franchise history (138).

I am not going to go over all of his high-level stats; we would be here for too long. But, you get the point. This Bold move, would be reviewed for years to come. It was 2009. Long gone were guys like Elway, Terrell Davis, Rod Smith, Ed McCaffrey...and now, Shanahan was no longer there to lead the team. At this point, I am...ahh...pretty bummed out.

In January 2009, Denver hired former New England Offensive Coordinator Josh McDaniels as their new Head Coach. At the time of his hiring, McDaniels was the youngest head coach in any of the four major North American professional sports and the fifth-youngest NFL head coach ever. This was a huge move; the move made me throw up in my mouth but it was a really big move. I hated New England and I didn't like the look of this guy. He looked and acted like he was 20 years old. Another big thing: he had to replace a legend: Mike Shanahan. But, real talk, it's just one of those things...sometimes you look at a person, and you just don't trust them. This was my feeling on Josh McDaniels.

McDaniels soon made me feel right about my decision to **not** like him. He made the decision to draft Tim Tebow from Florida and pick him in the first round. Many Scouts thought that Tim Tebow would be better suited as a Fullback or Tight End. Scouts also thought if he was drafted at Quarterback; a team should wait until the late 2nd or the 3rd or 4th rounds. But, McDaniels said - NOPE - he is my new starting Quarterback and I am using a high draft pick to get him. After a promising start to the season, the Broncos collapsed in epic fashion. After starting 6-0, the Broncos would then go on to win only 2 more games all year.

The Broncos now had a Quarterback room filled with guys like Brady Quinn, Kyle Orton, and yes... the most divisive Quarterback in the history of the NFL: Tim Tebow. They bizarrely had some success with Tebow at the helm...not much, but a slight amount. They won a playoff game with him as their go-to guy in 2011. There was a lot of luck involved per this one overall. They barely squeaked into the playoffs with a mediocre 8-8 record. The Steelers played an awful game and the Broncos found a way to win 1 (first round of the playoffs that year). But, no one, and I mean no one thought they had a high ceiling with Tebow at the helm (well other than Josh McDaniels).

The overwhelmingly majority of the population turned out to be right about that. McDaniels didn't last 2 years with Denver and Tebow didn't last as Denver's Quarterback. They, once again, needed to regroup and go in a different direction.

Chapter 9

2010's and beyond

John Fox was the Head Coach hired after Josh McDaniels departure; this was the standard move of an NFL franchise. You fail with a young, unknown offensive minded guy...you then bring in an older, more seasoned coach - a defensive guru who can lead you to the top. (or so you hope) It was 2011 and due to some poor performances recently, they had a very high draft pick. This was unusual for a very successful franchise like Denver. They had to make a decision on what to do near the top of the draft; no one quite knew the route they were going to take.

Per the 2011 Draft, A Quarterback was taken off the board 1st overall. Cam Newton: he had a great NFL carer and it would have been a hell of a pick for Denver. The Broncos needed a franchise Quarterback for their roster but they didn't feel one was available at #2 overall. They decided to go a different direction entirely and pick up a defensive stud: Edge Rusher / Poultry Aficionado, out of Texas A&M, Von Miller. He did not disappoint. As I already mentioned, the Broncos beat the Steelers in a playoff game recently (with Tim Tebow as their QB). Most, if not all, thought Denver was more lucky than good. Overall, they didn't quite have what it took to get to the highest level. So, they needed to do something different / something bold. They had a solid draft but needed to do something else.

I said most people a bit ago. There were still some that felt no changes were necessary. There were many experts and fans who thought they could run it back with similar talent and the same Quarterback (Tebow)...to attempt to get to the promised land. But Elway, their GM, and the collective braintrust thought differently and they made a move. A BOLD MOVE! They went after, and ended up acquiring, the legend: Peyton Manning.

Peyton Manning Years

There was a new hope as they brought in one of the best to ever do it. No more watching a 250 lb left hander throw ducks and miss Wide Receivers by 10 yards. But, the move to go after and get Manning: This was not a slam dunk. The Broncos had previously made the playoffs. As I said, they weren't lighting on the world on fire - they only went 8-8 and barely made it... but they made it. Getting rid of a beloved Quarterback like Tebow; then going after an old/oft-injured Quarterback like Manning...this was not a guarantee, far from it. Peyton Manning was coming off of multiple neck surgeries. These were not sprained ankles or wrists; some thought these were career-ending neck surgeries. There were many that thought Manning should retire at that point and not think about playing football anymore.

The early portion of the 2012 season did nothing to assuage those fears about Manning. He had some big-time struggles against poor opponents. He was pressing, he looked like he possibly lost arm strength, didn't appear as mobile, etc...and the team's play on the field just wasn't all that good. After 5 games, the Broncos were 2-3. This wasn't looking like the season that all had hoped for. Most were wondering if Peyton Manning had anything left in the tank. Many thought combining his age with all the injuries and surgeries...this would all be too much to overcome.

The thought process: Maybe he has had it, he should quit? OR...maybe he just needs a bit more time to get it together with teammates, with the coaching staff, needs more time learning the game plan, etc. It was the latter. Luckily, for all that cheer on the Orange and Blue...in Week 6, the Broncos put on an amazing offensive performance against the Chargers and they never looked back. They didn't only play well the remainder of the year...they won their last 11 games in a row.

All was right with the world again! The Broncos had found their go-to at the biggest position in all of sports. Jake Plummer had some nice years with Denver, but no one thought he was the man to lead them to the promised land. Everyone was excited about the team's prospects and all were thrilled with Peyton Manning!

As I said, after his first few games with Denver, fans were concerned. His injuries were nothing to take lightly; they were scary and many were worried he would ever play football again...let alone, at the high level he performed at, year after year with Indy. Manning actually stepped up his game, reaching new levels he hadn't reached before. The Broncos, under Manning's guidance, didn't just have a good year. They did so well; the team had a bye and they were riding high into the playoffs. The first game that year in the playoffs: they faced the Baltimore Ravens. But, they were at home, and all were thrilled. The Broncos were favored and rightfully so. Peyton and the offense played extremely well; but the Defense couldn't stop anything. Sadly, that beautiful season, which showed so much promise, came to an end. They didn't win 1 playoff game. It came to an abrupt end, but there was hope. Going in to this one; there were no guarantees. No one knew what to expect and they ended up having a great season with Manning as their QB. Peyton still looked to have a lot in the tank. They would run it back.

The next season was historic, or epic, as most people use nowadays (most people use epic too much nowadays). But this was a Burgundy style "big deal." The Broncos were absolutely incredible and were downright unstoppable on offense.

A Harbinger of things to come? Game 1: Manning led the Broncos on to the field for their 1st game of the 2013 NFL Season against the Super Bowl Champion Baltimore Ravens. The Broncos had lost in the year prior's playoffs and this was a big game for many reasons. It would obviously be a large challenge, playing the newly crowned Super Bowl Champs in the first game. How would the Broncs perform? Would Peyton Manning look spry or would he look like an old man? A this point, Manning is nearing 40 years old. We all know, at this point in an NFL or professional athlete's career, that has been filled with many injuries..the clock is ticking.

Soon, Manning would show he still had a bit of gas in the tank; I like sarcasm and am using "a bit" as an understatement here. Manning, against the Ravens that night, threw for not just 2 or 3 touchdowns or even 4...which would have been great. Manning threw for over 460 yards and 7 Touchdowns - in 1 game against 1 team; the defending Super Bowl Champs. That was unheard of. A 7 Touchdown performance has only happened a handful of times in NFL History. That passing performance is tied for the best game ever in the NFL! Manning showed he was not only good enough to perform as a high level QB. But, he proved he could be the best player in the league...yet again. (nearing 40 years of age)

It was a harbinger of things to come. The wins, during the 2013 season, kept piling up for the Broncos. Much like Limp Bizkit's amazing, iconic hit song, they just kept on rolling, rolling, rolling. The wins and the points would not stop; the Broncos weren't just winning games...they were embarrassing their opponents on a weekly basis. First 4 weeks of the season: Denver was 4-0. Their avg. per game, point totals vs. opponents: 44.75 points - 22.75 points. - those numbers are absolutely obscene. They were decimating their opponents. This looked like a high level College Football team beating up on D2 opponents. The next week: they travelled to Dallas to take on America's Team - 'dem Cowboys in Jerry-World. It was one of the most beautiful offensive performances in the history of the NFL. The final score was 51-48. From a Bronco's perspective, it wasn't great defense (obviously). But, the offense: they were playing at a level that no one had ever witnessed. As I mentioned, the Broncos were averaging just under 45 points per game, and after the Dallas game, and 5 games into the NFL Season...that number went up! Peyton Manning was on another level; he was in a league of his own, and this was the greatest sustained QB performance, anyone had ever seen!

The team, led by Manning, were incredible. They started the year: 9-1. They ended the regular season: 13-3. They were right where they wanted to be. The Broncos' 606 points (37.9 points per game) scored in the regular season is the highest total for any team playing a 16-game season. Throughout the regular season, numerous individual, league and franchise records were set, including Peyton Manning setting new NFL records for passing touchdowns and passing yardage, as well as the team setting new NFL records for touchdowns and points scored in a single season. Manning was named the MVP at the end of the year!

Playoffs 2013

After witnessing the most amazing season ever put together by an offense in NFL History, the expectations for Denver were through the roof. Due to their excellent performance, they garnered a 1st round bye. Jumping to Round 2 / Divisional Round: they beat the fertile Philip Rivers and the Chargers, in a better than expected game, from San Diego. A little too close for comfort - it was a close one but the Broncos still managed to pull it off.

Next Round: AFC Championship - this was an enormous game. They were not only in the AFC Championship. But, they were facing the vaunted New England Patriots. By this point, most people outside of the New England area, were very, very tired of the Patriots. With sustained winning, comes a lot of jealousy...and the Patriots for 13 years (and counting) were always at or near the top. They were led by the Darth Vader of the NFL Head Coaching circuit / Press Conference Low Talker / Hoodie McHooderson - Bill Belichick and the Golden Boy: Tom Brady. They were the #2 seed in the AFC that year and they were a team that no one wanted to face. The reason: they won games! All. The. Time. If they weren't in the Super Bowl, they were losing in the AFC Title Game, year after year...they were just that good. You had to respect them. And as a Broncos fan...or warm-blooded American outside of the New England area, hate them.

AFC Title Game vs. the Patriots

The Broncos did not have an issue in beating New England that day. They were up at halftime and by the end of the 3rd quarter, they were in complete control of the game: up 20-3. The Patriots were a team that had been decimated by injuries on offense leading up to that game and it showed. The Broncos didn't even put on a high-flying display; Peyton Manning mostly threw short pass after short pass, amassing a lot of yardage, and playing the clock game...the gameplay worked that day and the Broncos were on to the Super BOWL!

Super Bowl XLVIII

Led by Head Coach John Fox and Peyton Manning, the #1 seed in the AFC would be facing the other #1 seed (from the NFC), led by Head Coach Pete Carroll and Russell Wilson. There are a few phrases that come to mind when it comes to this game: "hard pill to swallow" or "one I'd rather forget," etc. etc. This was an absolute shit-show from start to finish for Denver. Early in the game, the Broncos Center snapped the ball so far over Peyton Manning's head, the ball ran all the way into the end zone: Safety and 2 points for Seattle. Not being able to get the snap from Center to QB, not a good thing... this was an indicator of things to come.

The Broncos had the greatest offense the league had ever seen in 2013. But, that day in New York in 2014, for the Super Bowl...it didn't show up and didn't live up to its billing whatsoever. The Broncos had the best offense...but Seattle's defense was also historic. Seattle (obviously) deserved the win and they took home the Lombardi trophy that day. This was sad for many reasons. Many thought the Broncos could run the table that year (undefeated season); that did not happen. Many thought they were unstoppable, as they were time after time, gamer after game, on offense. The saddest aspect of this one overall: This might be the end for Peyton Manning. And, we as Broncos fans, we have all watched this movie before. John Elway, the Franchise Legend - they won a Super Bowl and he, in perfect fashion, rode off into the sunset...retiring at the perfect time, for he and his legacy. Manning, due to age, and due to injuries...many thought this could be it for him. No one could blame him; he had done what few had done in the history of the NFL. By now, there were a large number of experts that believed he might be the GOAT. The Greatest Of All Time. (QB EDITION) Luckily, for not only Broncos fans...but the league in general - Manning had (at least) 1 more year in him! That was a large relief.

2015

The Broncos had been winning. They had not just been barely above average... they had been great and were near the top of the league. You don't luck your way into #1 seeds in the playoffs, and 13-3 records. They had been to the top of the mountain; but they had not found a way to win the big one in quite a while. So, in extremely surprising fashion, to all involved with the organization, they relieved John Fox of his head coaching duties. That was a high-level surprise. As I said, they weren't missing the playoffs and going 6-10...they were making it to Super Bowls. It was almost unprecedented to fire your coach after a Super Bowl appearance. But, they were daring and made the change. It was bold to go after Manning a few years prior; that worked...they figured they would try it again. Per the 2015 regular season, there were some major ups and downs.

Manning missed six games due to a partial tear of the plantar fascia in his foot and he had his worst statistical season since his rookie year. The Broncos had to go with a relative unknown, a young quarterback: Brock Osweiler. He filled in for Manning during a good portion of the second half of the regular season. Many were worried that Manning was about done. He had sustained yet another injury and it seemed, overall, injuries had really caught up to him. His stats absolutely fell off a cliff. He was, in football terms: an old man. There were many in Broncos kingdom that thought the team should ride it out with the newer, younger option: Osweiler...let him be the starter for the remainder of the year. Osweiler played fairly well for a period and the Broncos got some victories. Osweiler then ran into some struggles and major questions arose; Manning started to get healthier, and the staff decided it was best for the team to go back to the Legend.

Manning re-claimed his spot. But, the offense was just seemingly getting by. They were putting up points here and there, but it was quite a struggle. Luckily, under defensive coordinator Wade Phillips, the Broncos' defense was absolutely incredible. Led by Von Miller, Aqib Talib, Chris Harris, Demarcus Ware, and many others...they were the key contributors to winning week in and week out.

Denver watched what a great defense could do; Denver was previously crushed by Seattle in a Super Bowl (this was very recent history). So, they decided it was time they made it happen on the Defensive side of the ball. Stats on D: The Broncos ranked No. 1 in total yards, passing yards, average yards per rush and sack, and like the previous three seasons, the team continued to set numerous individual, league and franchise records. They were known as the "No Fly Zone." If you get a nickname as a Defense, that is saying something. Overall, this was quite a turn. In Denver, we had been use to watching Denver set records on offense. But, this year, the offense was letting them down - often. The Broncos defense performing wasn't just a nice thing; it was an absolute need!

The team finished the regular season with a 12-4 record. This was nothing to scoff at. But, they were kind of barely getting by game after game (in very close / nail-biting fashion). Fans were a bit underwhelmed, in that, they had been use to 45 point games and dominating blowouts...it just wasn't happening with this 2015 rendition of the squad. They were considered quite lucky to win many of those games and to have the 12-4 record going in to the playoffs.

Playoffs 2015

Based on other performances by the rest of the AFC, the Broncos were lucky enough to obtain a 1st round bye. It was needed. They needed to regroup and get healthy. The beat the Steelers in the divisional round; it was a similar blueprint that they used in the regular season...timely plays on offense, good solid defense and in the end, they won a close one. They would move on to the AFC Title game. They would face; who do you think? Of course, it was fricking New England. My goodness...they are ALWAYS there. Argh. Longer story short, the Broncos went up on the New England Patriots early...and they never looked back. This wasn't a blowout, not by any means. It was the same formula, the Broncos had been using over and over again to win games: Good Defense, a few timely plays on offense, and in the end, barely squeaking out a victory. But, a win in the NFL is a win; the Broncs were once again on the way to the Super Bowl!

Super Bowl 50! Date: February 7th, 2016 Santa Clara, CA

The Broncos made it a habit; they were finding ways to win. Whether it was Brock Osweiler leading their mundane offense, or the greatest, or one of the greatest of all time at the QB Position: Peyton Manning... they were winning games. They were now going to face a young, upstart Carolina Panthers squad, led by Cam Newton. Cam Newton / Von Miller were # 1 and # 2 in the draft only a few years prior. Those picks, by their respective organizations, obviously led to success as now the teams were meeting in the Super Bowl only a few years into their careers! Could one of the best defenses in history stop Superman? (as Cam Newton nicknamed himself).

Yes. Yes they could.

I talked of the picks in the draft a few years prior and how amazingly important they were. Cam Newton wasn't just a good player; he was the MVP in 2015. That year, he was the best in the league. No one was able to stop him. Game after game, he was not only passing the ball well...but defenses couldn't compete with his combination of size and speed running the ball. Going into the big game, Broncos fans were pretty worried. Those worries subsided shortly after the game started. The League's top defense: Denver, and their top pick from a few years back: Von Miller, were way too much for the Panthers to overcome. They stopped the Panthers at every turn, and frankly, this one was not even close. The game was never in doubt. The Broncos, were once again, Super Bowl CHAMPS! The Bronco's Von Miller was named Super Bowl MVP. Peyton Manning had done it; he had won another SUPER BOWL! The Broncos had done it again! Many labeled the game as boring. There wasn't much scoring and the game was never in doubt for

Denver. I don't care what many thought of the game. It was glorious and Denver was once again on top of the NFL world!

Chapter 10

A New Era

In 2012, Peyton Manning looked to possibly be done in the NFL. He was getting older and he was injured constantly. It looked to be the end of an era for one of the greatest Quarterbacks to ever lace them up. But, he proved all the analysts and skeptics wrong. Not only did he play again...he played at the highest of levels. He broke several passing records in his late 30's and he ended up winning a Super Bowl; not bad for a a slow-footed, old man with a bad neck. The Broncos were the champions of the league; and Manning was the guy that got them there. As a competitor, no one quite knew what the plan was next for Manning. Did the Broncos, and Manning, want to try and run it back...make it back-to-back Super Bowl Championships? After taking time to mull it over, a decision was made.

Manning announced his retirement, after 18 seasons, in early March 2016. The last words of his retirement speech were, "I've fought a good fight. I've finished my football race and after 18 years, it's time. God bless all of you and God bless football." As a Broncos fan, watching him on the Colts, I always admired him from afar. As a Broncos fan, watching him in Denver, we all knew he was a godsend...but, we all knew it wasn't going to last forever. No Broncos fan would trade what he did for the world. They had an amazing (albeit short) run with Manning as the leader of the squad.

Draft Picks / A New Direction

Following Peyton Manning's retirement, the Broncos underwent a process to select a new Quarterback throughout the entire off-season. The supposed heir-apparent: Brock Osweiler, spurned the Broncos, and decided he got a better deal from another squad: the Houston Texans. So, he was gone. They then decided to acquire Mark Sanchez in a trade with the Eagles. Sorry: I can't keep my food down thinking about that move - acquiring Mark Sanchez was questionable at best...and frankly pointless. The Sanchez move was just the tip of the iceberg. Trading for Sanchez wasn't smart but at least they didn't give up much in return for the guy.

But, per moves at the Quarterback position, it actually got worse. Any team who has been in the NFL for 30, 40 + years has had to make many draft picks. We all know 100% of them aren't going to be pro-bowlers. That is understandable. No one faults you for missing a pick here and there. "They can't all be winners" is the quote.

But the Broncos ramped that theory up...way up. The Broncos, in the 1st round of the 2016 draft, traded up, to acquire: Paxton Lynch - QB out of Memphis. There were many thoughts on what Paxton Lynch could do in the NFL. There were some positive assessments. There were also many, many negative reviews. Many thought he was at least 2-3 years away from being an NFL-Level Quarterback. But, hey Michael Jordan said: "You miss 100% of the shots you don't take." The Broncos took their shot. The Broncos were now without a go-to guy as their QB (Manning) and Bold moves have worked recently. They went bold again; they made their selection and drafted a 6'7" QB out of Memphis to lead the team into the future.

They now had a QB Room that consisted of: Mark Sanchez. Paxton Lynch. Trevor Siemian. Do you hear those other teams shaking in their boots? Yikes. The Broncos had some lean years with some mediocre Quarterbacks, but this was something extra special (and not in a good way). After seeing Peyton Manning for several seasons, and being used to watching greatness at that position: THIS.WAS.ROUGH. The Broncos defense carried them to some victories but the Broncos season was less than special overall and it was back to the drawing board.

The next few years, frankly, are barely worth mentioning. Super Bowl winning head coach Gary Kubiak retired. They tried new Head Coaches (Vance Joseph, Vic Fangio) and tried many Quarterbacks: Case Keenum, Joe Flacco, Trevor Siemian, Paxton Lynch, Teddy Bridgewater. A quick note on Paxton Lynch - he has struggled mightily in lower-level leagues like the CFL, the XFL and the USFL, but the Broncos drafted him in the 1st round to lead their NFL franchise. This was not one of their GM's shining moment picks.

2018 Draft

In 2018, the Broncos were struggling. They were a few years removed from a Super Bowl. Due to their poor performances, they were rewarded a top 5 Pick. The Broncos needs were obvious. They had more than one need overall; there is no doubt about that. But, a tried and true formula in the NFL is clear. First things first, make certain, you have the Quarterback position filled with someone who can win games and take you all the way. No one would ever question this formula. The Broncos appeared to be in luck this year at this draft.

As I have mentioned in the book already, the Broncos have made some questionable selections on draft day in the last decade. The 2018 Draft arrived, and as always, teams head's were filled with hope. The NFL has many, many experts dissecting team's every moves. But, frankly, you didn't have to be an "expert" to know what route the Broncos should take. Casual fans knew they NEEDED a Quarterback. It wasn't a nice to have; it was an absolute need. Case Keenum was a nice little pick-up. But, Case had been in the league for many years. His ceiling was quite low; he wasn't going to be a long-term solution at QB. Leading up to the draft, it was seemingly clear as to what the Broncos plans were. And, as I stated, the Broncos appeared to be in luck...this draft was filled with top-level QB Prospects. After the 1st round of this draft was completed, that was absolutely shown...5 guys were drafted in the 1st round. 5 selections at the QB position; that was a large number.

One in particular, per being connected to the Broncos, was mentioned over and over again before the Bronco's selection. Wyoming QB: Josh Allen was consistently mentioned, by a multitude of scouts, as a great fit for the Denver Broncos. He was not only a good height, but he looked to have the perfect QB build. He was a big athlete with a great arm; he was a great combination of not only arm talent, but also running the ball. In College, he got better, year after year. The only question: he needed a bit of time to develop as an NFL QB. The other question: would he even be there at the #5 selection? Most experts thought someone would select him before the Broncos would even get the chance. I was bummed; this guy seemed like he could be the next big thing for the Broncos. But now, in starting the draft, many scouts thought he would go 1, 2, or 3 overall. Keep in mind: the Broncos had not made a great selection, at the Quarterback position, since 1983. (Elway-Math says that is 35 years)

The draft commenced that day and there was a big surprise / huge surprise (Jean Claude Van Damme quote from Double Impact - one of the greatest unintentional comedy / action movies of all time) - anyway, back to it - Baker Mayfield was selected as the # 1 overall QB in this draft. He was the # 1 pick; he was going to the Cleveland Browns. Many thought he was too small and lacked the overall traits one needs to succeed as a QB in the NFL - not that ideal combo, to be selected as the #1 overall guy. But Cleveland didn't care and they selected him as the top selection of the whole draft. WHEW I thought... I liked to see that. Cleveland needed a guy; 99% of people thought they'd take a Quarterback, they did...but they selected a QB that most thought would be picked later in the 1st round or possibly even in the 2nd round. Maybe, Josh Allen to Denver...maybe this could work? #2 draft pick: Saquon Barkley goes to the Giants. Barkley - this guy is an absolute stud. No one faulted NY for taking him at #2. I didn't fault them either. I was thrilled. Josh Allen was still available!

The Commissioner came up, announced the next pick, said Quarterback - and my heart dropped - oh no, it's over, they are going to take him aren't they? The Jets selected Sam Darnold at #3. Most experts thought he'd be drafted #1. So, this wasn't a shock. Also...I was still pretty pumped up. There was still a chance for Denver to get "their guy." Now, I was thinking - it was almost a no doubt scenario. Cleveland had 2 picks in the top 4 selections; they already selected their QB at #1 overall and they wouldn't draft another Quarterback. This was all working out for Denver!!!! Cleveland selected CB Denzel Ward at #4.

HURRAH! YES! We made it; the Broncos now have a selection at #5! The Wyoming product, who had been playing next to Denver, right next to their

Scouting department and their GM...Josh Allen, right in their backyard, he would be the new Broncos QB and the unquestioned leader of the franchise for years to come. RIGHT??!?!??!?? I am popping champagne at this point. This was such a huge moment for a franchise that needed an injection of talent at the position. So, here it comes.

The Commissioner walked up to the podium and said, with the #5 pick, the Denver Broncos select: Bradley Chubb. Defensive End - North Carolina State. At this point, I was barely even listening to the draft because I thought it was a foregone conclusion that Denver was going to draft a QB. I thought they would draft the guy that was right in their backyard the whole time - Josh Allen. But, they did WHAT!??!!! WTF are you talking about? You have been given the wrong pick Commissioner Goodell (this was a hoax; it had to be). The Broncos didn't just do that did they? - That was it. That was the pick. John Elway and the other decision makers decided they needed to draft Bradley Chubb. Chubb had a nice year for a decent NC State team in College. His numbers were solid, but not spectacular. But, the Broncos appeared to see something in him and they decided that Bradley Chubb was their guy. Josh Allen was drafted by the Bills only 2 picks later. Lamar Jackson was still available as well; but the Broncs said F That... we are going with Chubb. We don't think a QB is necessary; we want to go with a solid defensive player and mediocrity at the position.

So...the Broncos rolled into next season at QB with Case Keenum, Kevin Hogan...you know, cream of the crop QBs. The season was...unsurprisingly, bad. They went 6-10 and they continued to toil in mediocrity for quite a while. Oh, and ah...update on how things have played out years late: Josh Allen and Lamar Jackson, at years end of the 2024 season...were fighting it out for MVP of the whole league. - Bummed out. Bradley Chubb isn't on the Broncos anymore - even more bummed out.

Chapter 11

Russell Wilson and Bronco's Front Office Moves

After years of seeing coaching by Vance Joseph and Vic Fangio, combined with poor Quarterback play from guys like Trevor Siemian, Case Keenum, Paxton Lynch, Brock Osweiler, Joe Flacco, Teddy Bridgewater, etc., the Broncos needed to do something different. Clearly, they couldn't figure out what to do in the draft. They needed to make a large splash move and look elsewhere. Fans were tiring of watching this team perform at a below average level for so long. At this point, the Broncos were many years removed from any kind of relevance. They hadn't even made the playoffs since their Super Bowl 50 Victory over Carolina. So, in March 2022, they made a massive, ground-breaking trade with the Seattle Seahawks. The Broncos pretty much gave them the farm, so to speak. Denver sent 2 1st round picks, 2 2nd round picks, a 5th round pick, and 3 players to Seattle for their Quarterback: Russell Carrington Wilson.

At that point, in March 2022, many were very excited and many were filled with HOPE! Not only did the Broncos make the move to acquire Russell Wilson...they signed him to a big, new extended contract - he was signed to a five-year, $242.6 million deal. Nearly all guaranteed (this wasn't just big, this was huge: near 250 MM is big enough, but all that guaranteed money...Broncos had better know what they're doing with this one)

Russell Wilson had been a really good quarterback for many years with Seattle. He was a Super Bowl wining Quarterback. He won that Super Bowl as a rookie; he was playing with an incredible defense that year... but still, the guy had shown he could do it in big moments.

In recent years, his play had waned slightly but he was still putting up solid numbers. The Broncos decision-makers decided they needed to be daring...so they got their guy. The Broncos now seemingly had a viable Quarterback to take them to the top of the league. During that time-period, it was consistently said the Broncos just needed a QB.

They were a good team, but not special...the missing piece, was a Quarterback. If they got one, that would be the final add to the puzzle and they would be back in Super Bowls again. So, this looked like the right move.

In 2022, it wasn't just a brand new QB that was going to come in and light the league on fire for the Broncos. They also hired a new Head Coach, after firing Vic Fangio. They brought in Nathaniel Hackett. (in typical league fashion: replacing a grizzled vet of a defensive coach with a younger offensive minded guy, it is like American Citizens voting for President)

Nathaniel Hackett, combined with Russell Wilson: most were excited about this marriage and where the Broncos could go with it! Nathaniel Hackett was not a hugely known coaching entity. But, he had certainly had some success. He had many great years wile attached with Aaron Rodgers; Nathaniel Hackett was known as a guy that could really help the Quarterback, and likely, in turn, could steer the offensive ship in the right direction.

The season would start in Seattle. Big Game: it was a matchup between Russell Wilson and his former Seattle Teammates. The Broncos were the huge favorite to win this game. Seattle had a brand new, young team with no-name players everywhere.

Wild Horses: A Denver Broncos Story

Many thought it would be an out and out embarrassment for Denver to lose this one, to such an underdog with their new, highly paid "star" Quarterback - Wilson. That embarrassment came to fruition. The Broncos played an awful game (especially on offense), the coaching was terrible, and they lost to the lowly Seahawks. 17-16. Seahawks fans were exuberant over the victory. (and they didn't appear to like Russell Wilson too much)

It was the opposite of a good start; it was not a good look. But, there is no need to walk to the ledge; it was the 1st game. At times, teams, players, and coaches need time to come together. Let's be positive; we will look at the game as an aberration. Week 2: The Broncos did win their 2nd game that year; they beat a team, that many considered, the worst team in the league - the Houston Texans - they beat them by a touchdown while playing in Denver. The Broncos finally scored a TD in the 4th quarter and won that one, barely against an awful-rebuilding Houston Texans squad. Week 3: the injured 49ers played extremely poorly in Denver and the Broncos won that game as well. Now, it was getting interesting; it was strange but interesting. The Broncos should be 0-3. Their offense was pathetic. The whole team didn't look great. But, no one will scoff at 2-1. So...onto the next.

Game 4 of the 2022 Season: The Broncos lost to the Raiders and looked bad in doing so. The Raiders were yet another poor team on the schedule and the Broncos found a way to lose to them by 9 points. Next: another below average team - the Colts. This game, game 5 of the season for Denver will be remembered. It will not be remembered for anything good - quite the contrary. It will be remembered as one of the worst games in NFL History. This was a Thursday night game in front of a prime-time audience. Matt Ryan and Russell Wilson battled it out and matched turnover for turnover and bad throw for bad throw; the teams matched punt for punt, and in the end, someone had to win...no one deserved it, but someone had to win and it was the Colts. 12-9 - in OVERTIME. The Broncos, with an overtime period, scored 9 G Damn points. SMH.

After 5 games into the regular season, you could at least pass a small amount of judgment. This was pretty bad. You cannot say, after 5 games, all was lost and that was it. But, after signing a so-called savior-level (possible MVP) Quarterback to the team...most were expecting more than an average of 13 points per game. Keep in mind - the Broncos had Peyton Manning years before that...in one season, after 5 games, the Broncos offense was averaging 45+ points per game. This was just a bit different (sarcasm again). Also, a reminder: they not only picked up a "great" Quarterback, but an offensive-minded head coach. The only thing offensive was their play on the field. Cheesy joke: but it was sitting right there, I had to use it. The rest of the season was **not** one for the ages. It was memorable in some regards. It was really memorable for 2 reasons.

Nathaniel Hackett: he was not ready to be the Head Coach of a 9 Man Football Team in the state of North Dakota. The guy was an absolute joke. I had stated he had a lot of success previously... being associated with Aaron Rodgers, year after year. There is a reason for that; Aaron Rodgers is really good at playing Quarterback. Talk about riding someone's coattails. This is that type of situation. Hackett seemed like a fun guy. Fun guys are fun to drink beers with at a TGI Fridays. That is not what you look for in a head coach.

LET'S RIDE

Let's Ride - That is my least favorite saying ever associated with the Denver Broncos... or frankly any sports team in any era.

Russell Wilson: all of a sudden - he really sucks at football. Also, let's be real. What a weird f'n dude. I mean, when he was out in Seattle... I obviously didn't pay much attention to the guy. But, the Broncos were now the laughing stock of the league and Nathaniel Hackett was a part of it. But, Russell Wilson was really the main culprit. This guy was originally known as Robot Russ, back in like 2017. For his teammates in Seattle, that was a way of calling him a guy with zero personality. He was a boring, milquetoast guy, who didn't share much and didn't really show much of anything. The guy calls himself Dangeruss. Time passed; he also, all of a sudden picked up an alter-ego, and he gave himself the moniker: Mr. Unlimited - look this sh%* up on Youtube and prepare to ask yourself: what the hell is wrong with this guy? This dude is corny AF. Shockingly corny. I could not believe it. I had heard some stories about Wilson...but I thought most of it was fabricated. My goodness...it is not. As a Broncos fan, I could take him being the biggest dork on earth. (and playing good football)

But now, we are watching this guy, play quarterback for the Broncos. He is not only himself: unlikeable and the opposite of charismatic, but he is also bleeding the Broncos dry of their money and their ability to pay other players. He was making so much money; he needed to be a high-level / top 5 performer at the position. He. Was. Not!

Anyway, the Broncos, one day after Christmas 2022, decided to fire their 1st year Head Coach: Nathaniel Hackett. The guy couldn't even finish off 1 full regular season before being fired. That day, December 26th: I was sitting around with family watching football and it was memorable for 1 reason. The game was a blowout; the Broncos looked like the worst team in the league and that led to Hackett's firing; they were absolutely destroyed by the mediocre Rams, led by Baker Mayfield (whom they only signed a few days before). Russell certainly helped push Hackett's firing forward with his awful play on the field; threw about 14 interceptions against the Rams that day. Wilson wasn't just bad; he was one of the worst quarterbacks in the league. I am not Warren Buffett but I do know this. If you pay heavily for a stock, you want to see peak performance. Russ: he was on the opposite level. Wilson was making nearly 50 million dollars per year to "play" quarterback for the Broncos. That year: Russell Wilson had a bottom 10 QB Rating in the league. That didn't even tell the whole story. If you dissect Russell and his performances, game after game, week after week, he was even worse than the actual stats showed. He missed so many open receivers and took so many unwarranted sacks. Let's just call it what it is. He was brutal and they were terrible. This was the opposite of what any Broncos fan wanted per this mega-deal for Wilson. After that vomit-inducing disaster, many people had a lot of explaining to do.

Chapter 12

Sean Payton / Hope for the Future

2023 had to be better right? Because, 2022 and Year One of the Russell Carrington Wilson Era - as Jim Lahey from Trailer Park Boys would say - that was an absolute shit-show. It would be shocking if this next season was worse. After trading for what you think is a top-level QB, and going 5-12, and having one of the worst offenses the league has ever seen (if it weren't for the last 2 games of the season, the Broncos would have broken records for all time futility) - all assumed it couldn't get worse. The Broncos could only go upwards and get better right? The 12 losses were tied for a Denver Bronco's NFL record season in losses. You get it; it was bad. Per 2022, Nathaniel Hackett - he was fired the day after Christmas. That

Christmas gift was a little late; but it was a gift nonetheless.

2023 rolled around and the Broncos hired a new Head Coach: Sean Payton. They / The Walmart Broncos paid a hefty sum for him (salary and a draft pick). But, as I always say: an NFL franchise, when seeing awful results with one coach, will always do the opposite with the next coach. The Broncos did just that. They hired a strict, disciplinarian for a Coach...a Coach who had proven himself at the highest levels to lead his franchise. Per this hire, I had varied feelings. I was a Broncos and Vikings fan and Payton played an integral role in Bountygate approximately 15 years ago. The Vikings were a part of that in a very negative way. Payton was brash and cocky; I didn't necessarily love the guy as a person. But, like most fans of most teams, and a SuperFan of Denver...you want a coach to come in and take the bull by the horns. After watching Hackett "lead" the previous year, something drastic needed to happen. In hilarious fashion, Payton didn't exactly have nice words to describe the Hackett Coaching era in Denver. Payton described Hackett's coaching job: "One of the worst coaching jobs in the history of the NFL" and said there were "20 dirty hands" around quarterback Russell Wilson's career-worst season that included just 16 touchdown passes and a league-high 55 sacks." Ultimately, Payton summed it up with "everything I heard about last season, we're doing the opposite." After seeing their performance on the field the year prior, Broncos fans loved that mindset.

It's understood. Payton wasn't too kind to Nathaniel Hackett nor was he high on anyone that played a part in the previous season. I was surprised Payton took the job frankly. He was the prime target of many teams as proven Super Bowl Head Coaches don't grow on trees. You had a team in Denver whose future looked pretty bleak. They didn't look to be special at any one position (outside of Surtain at Cornerback). And, at the most exceptional position: Quarterback, they looked to have the worst situation in the league. Russell Wilson was among the highest paid players in the league, yet his performance was near the bottom. This was not a winning formula. At this point, though he calls himself Mr. Unlimited...but he also is not a young dynamo. He is no doubt on the back-end of his career. At Quarterback, you usually want a certain type of player at the position: a Rookie playing on a very minimal contract who plays well enough so you can pay the rest of the team quite a sum, and you can win games that way. OR - you want a proven, high-level Quarterback who can take a team and win games, nearly on his own, with great performances put on his own shoulders...hence why the guy is making 50mm dollars per year. The Broncos were not a part of either formula...it wasn't even close.

2023 was an interesting journey. It wasn't a positively special year by any means. The Broncos seemed to have little hope. They had very few draft selections available before the season. Hmm? Why is that? Why is that? Oh yes...Russell F'n / High Knees Wilson.

Staying on that draft note: they couldn't build a team that way. There wasn't a ton of optimism heading into the season. Trying to find some positivity when the season started: you could tell Sean Payton knew what he was doing when it came to managing and running a team. He understood how many timeouts the team had in a half. He understood what a 2 minute drill was. He understood turning the ball over was bad. You know: Head Coaching 101 stuff...or at least I thought it was, but Nate Hackett was apparently unaware of some of these items.

Much like Al Bundy, I played High School Football. I was a Quarterback. Combining that with also possibly playing some college (I didn't, but I could have), plus watching the game and analyzing it since I was about 6 years old...I know when a QB is a potentially good performer and when a QB is the opposite.

Payton also did not give positive reviews of Wilson throughout the season. Though Russell Wilson put up better numbers in year 2 in Denver, Payton had major questions about him being able to lead as the franchise QB moving forward. Payton and the Broncos made a big decision fairly early on per the Russell Wilson experiment (an era that was supposed be long due to his large, extended contract). They decided to take it up the you know what...and release this awful quarterback, and do their best to rid themselves of this albatross on their franchise. George Paton and the Broncos signed this guy to a long-term, guaranteed contract... so this was no easy decision. But, if you are headed down a path this going nowhere...why keep going down that same path? Take a different one and hope and pray, though it is long and challenging, it will get better. Earlier, I mentioned, try to rid themselves; you can't fully do so as George Paton decided to give Wilson a long term extension and most of the salary was guaranteed. So, the Russell Wilson contract is the gift that keeps on giving (to him anyway), but as far as everyone else - it was a vampire, sucking the life out of the franchise continuously, and for quite a while.

If you're a Broncos fan and you don't despise Russell Wilson, you are a hell of a lot better person than I am. This guy came into the organization with an entourage surrounding him constantly and gobs of confidence. He then played some of the worst football I have ever seen and got paid 240 million plus dollars to do it!!!!!!!! I know people have said this before in other situations...but if I performed as he did in a Broncos uniform, I would give most of the money back.

Back to that 2023 Season - Near the end of the 2023 , Russell Wilson was benched. I was thrilled - Jarrett Stidham would now be the starter. I wasn't that excited about Stidham. I was just in the "Anyone but Wilson" camp. In fact, when it was announced: That was a celebratory moment; worthy of champagne and playing Trey Songz. That was as big of a gift as when the franchise axed Nathaniel Hackett less than a year prior. Russell Wilson was just that bad. People in sports media are interesting; I use the term interesting instead of saying infuriating. When Dangeruss had a job with Denver in Year 1, they were all ripping him to shreds at every turn. They were speaking of what an extreme dork he is, what a poser he is, and how awful his performances were, day after day, week after week. -they were right - across the board. But, at the end of year 2 of his awful tenure with Denver, the Broncos released him...and the media mostly had a pity party for the guy, talking of how he was doing better and gee whiz he tries so hard, and how the Broncos did him wrong. WOW! STFU.

You are kidding right? Do you listen to this guy (Dangeruss) talk? Did you watch the tape on this guy and his actual play on the field? He has 2 reads: he throws a check-down, for minimal yardage, then if his running back or Tight End catches it, Russ looks good as it is a completion and it helps bolster what his stats look like. His only other move is throwing the ball deep, and praying a big time Wide Receiver makes a big time play. There is no in-between with this guy and defenses understood it. He got old quickly; he could no longer run the ball either. He was just flat out awful. Plain and simple. In terms of salary at the quarterback position, he should have been paid at the bottom 15% level of the league. Instead it was opposite, and that set the Broncos back. That trade with Seattle: what an awful decision. This was one of the worst trades and salary moves in NFL history. This was up there with the Herschel Walker trade of 1990. MR. Unlimited / High Knees / Dangeruss / the creepy guy who puts himself on a pedestal and is all about his brand...moved on to the Pittsburgh Steelers the next season. He would now be their problem. Good riddance to one of the least likable players in the history of the franchise. I like Bill Romanowski more than Wilson. That is saying something.

What Now?

After thinking, only 2 years ago, the Broncos found their guy at QB and the team was now set. It was, once again, back to the drawing board. The Broncos were now nearly 10 years removed from the Super Bowl. They not only, weren't performing at the highest levels, they couldn't even make the playoffs. They actually were #2 - for the longest drought not making the playoffs by any franchise as of 2024. But, the 2024 Draft was coming and the Broncos did actually have a pick. George Paton, and the other braintrust, didn't give this pick away to Seattle. So, that was good.

But, #12 overall, you are kind of in a tough slot, per this draft, if looking to solve the quarterback problem. By the time the Broncos select, the top Quarterbacks will all be gone. Knowing, you need to fill the #1 position in all of sports and are likely not going to be able to anytime soon...it's not a great feeling. Plus, because of that Russell Wilson trade, they don't have a lot of draft capital or salary, to do a lot of wheeling and dealing (thanks again Mr. Unlimited).

The draft started and QBs were going off the board at a high rate. This was not good. Due to that, the hope is the Broncs get a great player and go a different direction overall. The Commissioner gets to #12, and states, the Denver Broncos select: Quarterback...I thought, who is left? Teams have already taken 5 QBS in the first 10 picks. That is a lot. Unfortunately, the odds don't stack in the favor of all of these guys performing well. So, with the Broncos also deciding to make a move to go that same route...also selecting a QB - this would make the 6th Quarterback selected in the first 12 picks. This will, very likely, not work out. At that 12th pick, they selected Bo Nix - QB - out of Oregon. The large majority of scouts and experts thought he could be okay. Per scouts, and experts, the thought was Nix might get drafted in that 35-50 range overall. So, this pick looked to be a bit of a stretch... taking him at 12. But, I can honestly say it - Sean Payton has made many good moves. So, we shall see.

New Era, New Hope and a Path Forward

The 2024 season started with some optimism. You have a coach in place; a proven head coach who has plans and seems to have a vision to guide the team in the right direction. I don't think anyone thought the Broncos were going to light the world on fire.

But, it is almost like that "new car" sense; before you drive it off the lot, there is a lot of unfulfilled value there. Whenever a rookie, especially a rookie Quarterback, joins the squad - you are filled with this thought: the likelihood is that the guy won't turn out, but since you don't know for certain, there has to be a sense of hope. Bo Nix was a 24 year old that played for multiple college teams. 24 is obviously not old in life, but it is kind of old in terms of being drafted as a Rookie in the NFL. Nix is considered a polished/experienced player. I like that. I would rather see experience over the favorite buzzword of all NFL teams around draft time: "potential." You usually, at least, kind of know what you're getting. The scouting report on him was that he was the 6th best Quarterback coming out for the draft, maybe even lower than that. Scouts essentially said, what you see if what you're going to get...meaning, he has a fairly low ceiling and he really won't get much better than he is right now. He was really good in College. But that doesn't translate to the NFL.

In 2024, the Broncos didn't just perform well under Nix, they exceeded exceptions. Very few expected a winning season. They not only did that, but they made the playoffs. It was a short lived playoff run but they made it happen...nonetheless. One season in with Bo Nix: he is the best the Broncos have had at the position since Manning left in 2015. High praise - yes? Too much praise, too soon? Yes. But, per assessments of his performance, that is the truth.

It is Q1 2025...so, you can't say he is a no-doubt Franchise Star. But, based on the players at the position over the last 10 years, there has to be some hope. I am not, by nature, an optimistic guy in a lot of ways. I am also an extreme realist when it comes to Denver and how they do business. Per drafted QBs in the modern era - see Tim Tebow, Paxton Lynch, Brock Osweiler, Drew Lock...you get the picture. These were guys that let everyone in Broncos' nation down. Bo has picked the fanbase up again. It is now the offseason. And the biggest win??? Instead of the Broncos talking about who they can go after to play Quarterback for the team (yet again) this offseason...they are talking of free agent pickups and draft picks to supplement what they already have at the position. As an NFL Franchise, this is exactly where you want to be.

The Broncos have a good defense, a great Coach and a damn good QB who looks to have a bright future. The vibes in the Mile High City are positive and we are all excited for next steps in this journey. There is no doubt about it; Manning and Elway are missed and people still talk about them, a lot, to this day. Can Bo Nix make people talk about them less and less? That is the Million Dollar Question; that is the hope of Broncos fans across the globe. There is another great and positive thing about this story moving forward for Denver - in no way, will it ever again include Russell F'n Wilson.

Printed in Dunstable, United Kingdom